OUR WORLD
101 Facts About
101 Facts About

101 FACTS ABOUT

OCEANS

Julia Barnes

Gareth Stevens Publishing
A WORLD ALMANAC EDUCATION GROUP COMPANY

Please visit our web site at: www.garethstevens.com
For a free color catalog describing Gareth Stevens Publishing's
list of high-quality books and multimedia programs,
call 1-800-542-2595 (USA) or 1-800-387-3178 (Canada).
Gareth Stevens Publishing's fax: (414) 332-3567.

Library of Congress Cataloging-in-Publication Data available upon request
from publisher. Fax (414) 336-0157 for the attention of the Publishing
Records Department.

ISBN 0-8368-3709-6

This North American edition first published in 2004 by
Gareth Stevens Publishing
A World Almanac Education Group Company
330 West Olive Street, Suite 100
Milwaukee, WI 53212 USA

This U.S. edition copyright © 2004 by Gareth Stevens, Inc. Original edition © 2003 by First
Stone Publishing. First published by First Stone Publishing, 4/5 The Marina, Harbour
Road, Lydney, Gloucestershire, GL15 5ET, United Kingdom. Additional end matter © 2004
by Gareth Stevens, Inc.

First Stone Series Editor: Claire Horton-Bussey
First Stone Designer: Rob Benson
Geographical consultant: Miles Ellison
Gareth Stevens Editors: Catherine Gardner and JoAnn Early Macken
Cover photo: Lloyd West

Photographs © Oxford Scientific Films Ltd

Printed in Hong Kong through Printworks Int. Ltd

1 2 3 4 5 6 7 8 9 07 06 05 04 03

The oceans contain some of the last unsolved mysteries on Earth. The ocean floor is so deep in some places that only in recent years have scientists been able to explore it.

Deep under the water, scientists have found a fantastic landscape of flat land, deep valleys, and tall mountains that is even more spectacular than the scenery we see on land.

At one time, people thought that no form of life could survive at such incredible depths. Now, we know that an unusual variety of fish live on the ocean floor.

We must make good use of this knowledge to protect not only these newfound deep-sea creatures but all the wonderful forms of life that live in and around the world's oceans.

OCEANS OF THE WORLD

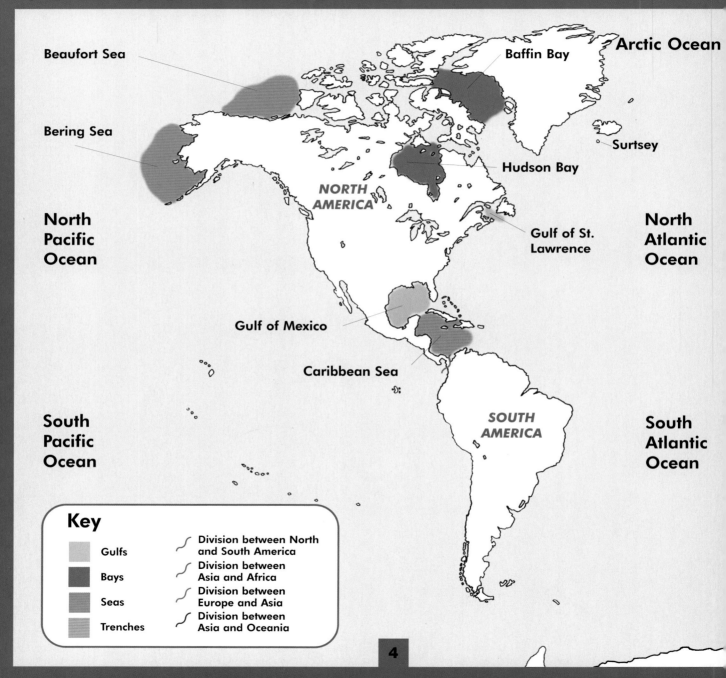

Beaufort Sea

Bering Sea

Baffin Bay

Arctic Ocean

Surtsey

Hudson Bay

NORTH
AMERICA

Gulf of St.
Lawrence

North
Pacific
Ocean

North
Atlantic
Ocean

Gulf of Mexico

Caribbean Sea

South
Pacific
Ocean

SOUTH
AMERICA

South
Atlantic
Ocean

Key

Gulfs

Bays

Seas

Trenches

Division between North
and South America

Division between
Asia and Africa

Division between
Europe and Asia

Division between
Asia and Oceania

Norwegian Sea

Barents Sea

Arctic Ocean

Kara Sea

Laptev Sea

East Siberian Sea

North Sea

White Sea

Bering Sea

Baltic Sea

EUROPE

Black Sea

ASIA

Sea of Othotsk

Sea of Japan

North Pacific Ocean

Aegean Sea

Persian Gulf
Gulf of Oman

Yellow Sea

Mediterranean Sea

AFRICA

Andaman Sea

East China Sea

South China Sea

Mariana Trench

f of nea

Arabian Sea

Bay of Bengal

Arafura Sea

Red Sea

Indian Ocean

Gulf of Siam

OCEANIA/ AUSTRALIA

Coral Sea

South Pacific Ocean

Barrier Reef

Gulf of Aden

Timor Sea

Antarctic (Southern) Ocean

Great Australia Bight

Tasman Sea

ANTARCTICA

1 Water covers so much of the surface of Earth that it looks like a blue ball from distant space. In fact, more than two-thirds of our planet is underwater.

2 Only a little bit of all Earth's water is in rivers, lakes, and frozen icecaps. Most of it is the salt water of the mighty oceans.

3 Most of Earth's water forms three separate but connected oceans. They are the Pacific, Atlantic, and Indian Oceans.

4 Mapmakers sometimes mark two other oceans: the Arctic Ocean, around the North Pole, and the Antarctic, or Southern, Ocean, near the South Pole.

5 The oceans contain bays, or small areas of water partly surrounded by land, and gulfs, which are similar to bays, but bigger and deeper.

6 Bodies of salt water that are smaller than oceans are called seas. They include the Caribbean and the Mediterranean Seas.

7 Some of these bodies of water are warm. In the water of the Persian Gulf, for example, temperatures can reach 97° Fahrenheit (36° Celsius).

8 Some seas contain very cold water. The White Sea on the northern coast of Russia drops down to an icy 28° F (-2° C).

9 Although we cannot drink the salty seawater, we still could not live without the oceans.

10 Oceans help to supply freshwater, the kind of water humans can drink. Freshwater comes from rivers and lakes and starts as rain or snow.

11 The Sun heats the ocean, and the water **evaporates**, forming clouds of **water vapor**. As the clouds travel over land, the water returns to Earth as rain or snow.

12 Without this source of water, animals, plants, and people could not survive on Earth.

13 In many countries around the world, fish are an important source of food (right).

14 Oceans have been part of the planet since life began, but the world looked very different millions of years ago.

15 Today, we are used to seeing the map of the world divided into seven continents, or giant land masses.

16 Scientists think that about 1.5 billion years ago, Earth had only one huge supercontinent.

17 Both the land and the ocean floor were part of a thin layer of rock, called the crust, that floated on **magma**, or liquid rock.

18 The movement of the magma grew so powerful that the crust cracked into huge pieces, called plates.

19 As the plates inched apart, the magma pushed up through the cracks to Earth's surface.

20 As the magma cooled, it hardened into solid rock. Water flowed into the lower surrounding areas to form the oceans and seas.

21 Over millions of years, the single huge continent broke into smaller pieces to form the world as we know it today.

22 If you take a close look at a map, you can see that the seven continents might still fit back together, like pieces of a giant jigsaw puzzle.

23 All the plates keep shifting very slowly. The

continent of North America creeps away from Europe at the rate of about 1 inch (2.5 centimeters) every year.

24 As the plates shift, the Atlantic Ocean (left) grows slightly wider. The Pacific Ocean slowly becomes smaller.

25 Under the depths of the oceans, tall peaks and great valleys create landscapes even more amazing than some of the most dramatic scenery on the land.

26 The **continental shelf** is a ledge around the edges of the continents. It reaches out to where the water is about 660 feet (200 meters) deep.

27 From the continental shelf, the ocean floor slopes down steeply to the **abyssal plain**, which is 3.5 miles (5.6 kilometers) beneath the surface.

28 Huge mountains and deep **valleys** break up the plain. Where Earth's plates are pulling apart, long mountain ranges have formed.

29 The ocean's tallest mountains break the surface of the water as islands. The deepest valleys, called trenches, plunge to incredible depths.

30 The tallest ocean mountain is in the water between Samoa and New Zealand. This peak climbs up about 28,500 feet (8,687 m) from the floor of the ocean.

31 The Mariana Trench, in the northwest Pacific, is the deepest part of

of the ocean. It extends down about 36,200 feet (11,033 m).

32 The Mariana Trench goes down about as deep as Mount Everest, the world's tallest mountain, extends to the sky.

33 There are more **volcanoes** under the sea than on the land because the crust on the ocean floor is thinner.

34 A huge circle of underwater volcanoes, called the Ring of Fire, surrounds the plate under the Pacific Ocean.

35 Many underwater volcanoes remain active, or able to erupt. In 1963, a volcano erupted out of the sea near Iceland and created a new island, named Surtsey (above).

36 In the ocean depths below 20,000 feet (6,100 m), the water is dark and freezing cold.

37 Enormous water pressure makes it difficult to explore the depths of the oceans.

38 Using special submarines, called submersibles, people have begun to learn about the deepest parts of oceans.

39 At least two hundred **species** of fish live in the depths of the oceans, and scientists find more varieties every year. Many deep-sea fish, such as the ratfish (left), have unusual shapes or features.

40 Light does not reach down very far into the ocean water. Some creatures of the deepest parts of the ocean can make their own light to lure their **prey** or protect themselves.

41 The anglerfish, which can be smooth (right) or tasselled (above left), produces a light that looks like a torch. The light hangs over its mouth.

42 Other fish are attracted by the anglerfish's light, and they swim right into its mouth.

43 The flashlight fish has a light just above its eyes that it can turn on and off. The most powerful light produced by any living creature, it can be seen from 100 feet (30 m) away.

44 Flashlight fish use their lights so that they can swim together as a **shoal**. If an enemy approaches, they switch off their lights and escape into the darkness.

46 In the shallower parts of seas and oceans, plants can grow in the **seabed**. More kinds of animals live closer to the water's surface, too.

45 Even water plants need light in order to grow. Plants cannot grow at the deepest levels of the ocean floor.

47 Billions of plankton, or microscopic plants and animals, make the main meal for many different ocean animals.

48 Some animals are **predators** that hunt for food. Others eat plants from the seabed.

49 The ocean is home to blue whales (left), the largest and heaviest animals on Earth. One blue whale can weigh 150 tons, which is about as much as thirty elephants. It can be 100 feet (30 m) long.

50 Blue whales eat plankton and krill, tiny shrimplike animals that are among the smallest creatures in the sea.

51 Whales may look like fish, but they are **mammals**, which need to breathe air. To take a breath, they must swim to the surface of the water.

52 As a whale exhales, or breathes out, a huge spray of water shoots up from the surface (below).

guides it to the surface of the water so that it can breathe.

55 Dolphins are the acrobats of the oceans. They can perform fantastic leaps and twists high over the water (above) and swim up to 25 miles (40 km) an hour for short distances.

53 Dolphins are also ocean mammals. They live in groups that hunt, swim, and play together. Sick or injured dolphins are cared for by the group.

54 When a dolphin is born, its mother

56 Dolphins hunt for fish by making a clicking sound that travels through the water.

57 When a dolphin's clicking sound hits some fish, an echo bounces back to the dolphin. The echo tells the dolphin where food might be.

59 The great white shark (below) has a healthy appetite. It eats dolphins, seals, turtles, birds, other kinds of sharks, and trash tossed by boaters.

58 More than three hundred species of sharks live in oceans around the world. With powerful bodies and razor-sharp teeth, most sharks make fierce predators.

60 The whale shark is the world's biggest fish, reaching 40 feet (12 m) in length. Like some of the big whales, this shark lives on a diet of tiny plankton and small fish.

61 Other big residents of the ocean are manta rays (left), wide fish with flat bodies and winglike fins. Manta rays can weigh more than one ton, and they can be 20 feet (6 m) across.

62 Manta rays live in the upper part of the ocean, but many other members of the ray family live on the seabed, where they eat clams and oysters.

63 Ocean creatures have developed a wide variety of ways to hunt their prey, defend themselves from predators, hide from danger, and survive in their watery world.

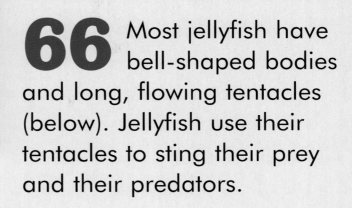

66 Most jellyfish have bell-shaped bodies and long, flowing tentacles (below). Jellyfish use their tentacles to sting their prey and their predators.

64 The octopus uses its eight long arms, called tentacles, to grip its prey. When in danger, it sends out a jet of inky fluid.

67 People who swim in the warm waters of Australia and Hawaii must watch out for box jellyfish, which have a deadly sting.

65 The blue-ringed octopus (above) is only about the size of a golf ball, but this small creature has a deadly poison in its bite. It lives and hunts in shallow coral and rock pools around Australia.

68 The lives of ocean animals are joined. One may be a predator, and another may be its prey.

69 In a more unusual kind of relationship, animals help each other. For example, a small fish works as a "cleaner," and a big fish is the "customer."

70 Cleaner fish (below) swim around their

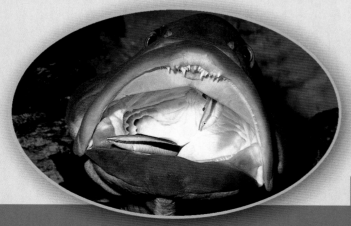

customer, picking off dead skin and tiny bloodsucking pests called parasites.

71 The cleaner fish earn rewards for their work. Big fish carry around a load of parasites, which cleaner fish eat.

72 Customers do not attack the cleaners. They are glad to get rid of the pesty parasites.

73 Cleaners, such as banded shrimps, even enter the jaws of sharks to clean their teeth.

76 Angelfish, clownfish, and butterfly fish (below) are among the most spectacular fish in the ocean.

74 One-quarter or more of all the animals that live in oceans can be found in the warm, shallow water around **coral reefs** (above).

77 Coral looks like a plant or a rock, but it is made of thousands of tiny animals called polyps.

75 About two thousand different kinds of fish live around coral reefs. They are many different shapes and sizes. Some are brightly colored.

80 Some animals live mainly on the land, but they are equally at home in the ocean's water.

78 When a polyp dies, it leaves behind a hard skeleton. New polyps grow on top of the skeletons. Eventually, a colorful coral reef grows up from billions of polyps.

79 The biggest coral reef is the Great Barrier Reef off the east coast of Australia.

81 Seals and sea lions can be clumsy on land, but they are super swimmers. They can dive to a depth of 1,000 feet (305 m) and stay underwater for thirty minutes.

82 Near Arctic waters, the seals' chief enemies are polar bears (above), the world's biggest four-legged **carnivores**.

83 Seals poke their heads up out of holes in the ice to breathe. Polar bears wait and watch for them.

84 Most penguins (below) live along the frozen coast of Antarctica in huge groups, which are called colonies.

85 Emperor penguins, the world's biggest swimming birds, may grow to be nearly 4 feet (1.2 m) tall. They can weigh about 66 pounds (30 kilograms).

86 The water in oceans is never still. Cold and warm **currents** move under the water's surface.

87 When the wind blows across the sea, it makes ripples on the surface of the water. If the wind keeps blowing, the ripple gets bigger and forms a wave.

88 Some waves travel all the way across the ocean before they crash on a shore.

89 A wave can tower more than 40 feet (12 m) high, which is bigger than a two-story house.

90 A **tidal wave**, or **tsunami**, causes a lot of damage on shore.

91 The biggest **tsunami** ever recorded peaked at 210 feet (64 m), which is higher than a ten-story building.

92 Along the coastline, the level of the sea changes during the day. As the Moon moves around Earth, the water level stretches up the beach and then retreats back down.

93 When the water is at its highest point on the beach, it is said to be at high tide.

94 At low tide, water pulls back to the sea and exposes the beach, which may include rocks and shallow pools (above).

in the oceans, which causes **water pollution**.

97 Sometimes, a big oil tanker crashes on a rock, and the oil leaks out to sea. The oil coats and kills the animals and birds that live on the shore and pollutes the water.

95 Although they are home to a wonderful range of plant and animal life, the world's oceans are in danger today.

96 People dump harmful waste

98 Modern methods of fishing (left) allow people to catch a huge number of fish in nets that can be 1 mile (1.6 km) long. Now, certain kinds of fish are becoming rare.

99 Beautiful coral reefs are also in danger. Careless divers or boat drivers can damage a fragile reef. Some people even remove coral to make jewelry.

100 Coral reefs are home to so many different kinds of life that some scientists think reefs may be as important to Earth's health as the world's rain forests.

101 Without oceans, life could not exist on land. We should look for ways to protect our oceans and to stop the damage and the pollution.

Glossary

abyssal plain: a large, flat area of the ocean floor.

carnivores: meat eaters.

continental shelf: a narrow ledge where the water meets the land.

coral reefs: areas close to the surface of an ocean that are made of tiny sea creatures.

currents: powerful movements of air or water.

evaporates: changes from a liquid to a vapor.

magma: red-hot, liquid rock that lies beneath Earth's crust.

mammals: warm-blooded animals that need to breathe air.

predators: animals that hunt other animals for food.

prey: animals that are hunted by other animals for food.

seabed: the ground at the bottom of an ocean or sea.

shoal: a school, or group, of fish that swim together.

species: types of animals or plants that are alike in many ways.

tidal wave: a huge, destructive wave caused by an underwater earthquake, volcano, or strong wind; also called a tsunami.

tsunami: a tidal wave.

valleys: low-lying flat areas.

volcanoes: mountains that build up after eruptions of red-hot, liquid rock from beneath Earth's crust.

water pollution: human-made waste that makes water unhealthy and dirty.

water vapor: water that has evaporated into the air.

More Books to Read

***First Encyclopedia of Seas and
Oceans***
Ben Denne
(Usborne)

Life in the Oceans
Lucy Baker
(Two-Can)

***Ocean (Eye Wonder* series)**
Sue Thornton and Samantha Gray
(DK Publishing)

***Oceans (Make It Work!* series)**
Barbara Taylor
(Creative Publishing)

Web Sites

Biomes of the World
mbgnet.mobot.org/

The Earth's Oceans
www.zoomschool.com/
subjects/ocean/

Oceans Alive!
www.abc.net.au/oceans/alive.htm

Ocean World
oceanworld.tamu.edu/index.html

To find additional web sites, use a reliable search engine to find one or
more of the following keywords: **coral reef, oceans, Pacific Ocean.**

Index